Want Priority Access to FREE eBooks Additional Materials for this Book?

As we release NEW eBooks, we offer them for FREE for a limited time. You will be the FIRST one to know when they are FREE. Join 1000's of insiders who are getting access to FREE Kindle book promotions weekly.

Click HERE for FREE additional material and FREE eBooks-
www.rictamilypublishing.com

Table of Contents

Introduction: Just Cracking the Surface

Chapter 1: An Invitation to Dissent, and a Call to Serve

Chapter 2: Two for the Price of One

Chapter 3: Decision 2008 and the Cracked Ceiling

Chapter 4: When the Arab Spring was Sprung?

Conclusion: 2016 and Beyond

Review Link

Preview of "Become an Online Entrepreneur"

Check Out My Other Books

Dedication

Disclaimer

Introduction
Just Cracking the Surface

Hillary Rodham Clinton. When we hear that name a lot of things come to mind. But who is she? This has been a question that the American public has been asking itself ever since she rose to national prominence. It was obvious from the beginning of the her husband's 1992 Presidential campaign that she was destined to be much more than just a "first lady", and as Bill Clinton himself famously quipped, it was, "Two for the price of one". Because Hillary has always been just as formidable of a political player as her husband ever was.

Hillary's' life spans many trials and triumphs stretching all the way back to her days at Wellesley College where she first stormed the national stage when she was chosen to deliver what turned out to be a very profound and thought provoking commencement speech. Although only 22 years old at the time, this speech spring boarded her into what would be a life of political and social activism. She developed a laser focus that would last her through her tenure at Yale Law School, The Governor's Mansion of Arkansas, and then the Whitehouse with Bill Clinton.

And Hillary is still plotting her course. She served two terms in the Senate during New York's darkest 9/11 hour. And then she made history again as the first woman to run for President in 2008, a major feat that went almost unacknowledged due to Hillary's sheer political power and steady rise to ascendancy, but it was a historic first nonetheless. And even though as she said in her concession speech to Barak Obama, that she had not managed to crack that final, "Glass Ceiling", she maintained that she had her supporters had managed to, "Put a Million Cracks in it".

Love her or hate her, Hillary is right, she is a pioneer and a trailblazer, even her supposed Republican opponent Sarah Palin paid her this homage back in 2008, and the rest of the country should too. Because Hillary Clinton represents the determination of the American spirit and as we look to 2016, even though some try to write her off as the politics of the past, deep down Hillary Clinton's commitment to this country is a breath of fresh air. And as she almost succeeded in breaking that final glass ceiling, we find that even though most of us thought we already knew Hillary Clinton, we were really just cracking the surface.

Chapter 1
An Invitation to Dissent, and a Call to Serve

In the spring of 1969 when Hillary gave the first major public speech of her life, she was not the finely tuned mouthpiece of the Clinton machine that we know today. On May 31st 1969 she was just one undergrad among many at Wellesley College. When asked about this pivotal moment Hillary recalls being both exhilarated and incredibly anxious that her classmates had chosen her for this very special task.

Even back then Hillary was breaking major ground, because she was the very first student to be allowed to give a commencement speech at Wellesley. The decision to allow a student to speak resulted from a last minute suggestion by the college president Ruth Adams. She gave the go ahead and asked the student body who they would like to represent them, and without hesitation they chose Hillary. The end result was a young Hillary Rodham standing bold and defiant giving a passionate, seven minute long, call to action. In her speech she emphatically encouraged her classmates to protest, demonstrate and use any other means of civil dissent at their disposal, in order to criticize unjust laws and government practices.

Before you decide that Hillary was just another radical among radicals, keep in mind the year that she was championing this kind of open dissent. It was 1969 and although man had landed on the moon, there were thousands of young people dying every day in a Vietnam War that most didn't agree with or even understand the basis for. She charged her classmates to take matters into their own hands even though they were young, and lacked the political power and capitol to write the laws, she implored them to protest and carry out what she termed there, "indispensable task of criticizing" the government. When no other means of change was available, the young Hillary was a firm believer in taking it to the streets.

This famous invitation to dissent that Hillary intoned to her fellow classmates in her 1969 commencement speech at Wellesley College, has led for many to try to nail her down as a radical. But that is a mostly unfair criticism. You have to keep in mind the turbulent times that she lived in when she spoke those words. As shocked as we are today to hear of a destroyed CVS and night of rioting in Baltimore Maryland, as bad as that is, the summer of '69 saw rioting and protests on a much more massive and destructive scale than anything this country has witnessed in recent years. So, you have to understand the context of the conversation she was having with these students, these turbulent times were their life, this is what they lived and breathed on a daily basis.

And Hillary herself has maintained that she left any possible radical leanings when she left Wellesley. She did hang onto her interest in social justice though and soon became an active member on the board of the "Yale Review of Law and Social Action". Although not radical in nature, this board was proactive and their stated goal was to, "Present forms of legal scholarship and journalism which focus on programmatic solutions for social problems". She had a built in drive of service and helping those in need. Hillary was always much more of a nurturing spirit than a destructive one.

This drive to help the downtrodden and the less advantaged has been a theme that she has embraced for much of her career. And it was the plight of disadvantaged children that would take the center stage of her activism early on. Immediately after obtaining her law degree her first major gig as an attorney was as a staff attorney for the "Children's Defense Fund" in Cambridge Massachusetts. It was here that she exerted enormous amounts of her energy in launching the CDF's famous report, "Children out of School in America"

It was this report from the CDF that sent Hillary literally banging down the doors of Massachusetts to figure out why so many children were not enrolled in school. As part of a nationwide survey she went door to door to seek these so called, "missing students" out. The results of her report were stunning; a large majority of the children that were labeled as "missing" were actually displaced due to disabilities that left them unable to attend classes. After receiving this revelation, the data from they survey was sent directly Washington where after congressional debate, major legislation was enacted to finally ensure that these children could go to school and have their needs met.

The results of this survey helped to spur on a movement to make all school facilities accessible to the disabled. Hillary has always been inspired to help the disenfranchised and she has always had a special heart especially for children. As one of her inspirations for this cause, she often sites the troubled childhood of her own mother. Like something straight out of the little orphan Annie's "hard knock life", the tale of Dorothy Rodham is enough to make you cry, but it also served as a testimony to the young Hillary how the disadvantaged can rise up from their hardship.

The things that Dorothy Rodham had to deal with were truly tragic. She was born into a troubled home; her father was the alleged victim of domestic violence from her own mother. As rare as documented cases of men suffering from domestic violence are, this is one that was seemingly verified in the courts of 1926, where even Dorothy's Aunt, her mom's own sister, bore eye witness testimony in court to the disturbance between her parents, stating that, "She had a violent temper and flew at him in a rage, and would fight him." The court also further documents instances where Dorothy's father was scratched and even punched in the face by his wife.

This was the volatile landscape that Hillary's mom had been born into, but as bad as things were they were about to get worse, because in light of the court's ruling over the issue of domestic violence perpetrated by Dorothy's mom, she was declared an unfit mother, and after further legal battles and a prompt divorce, Dorothy was shipped off from her Chicago birthplace to live in California with her unsympathetic and unwelcoming grandparents.

To say that the grandparents were unenthusiastic adoptees would be an understatement, they viewed Dorothy as an unwanted burden that they shouldn't have to deal with. Dorothy described her grandfather as remote and detached while her grandmother was an extreme and often harsh disciplinarian. In one particularly cruel stroke, Dorothy's grandmother found that she had snuck out to go trick or treating on Halloween, a holiday that the Grandparents forbid celebrating on religious grounds. The punishment was swift and severe. Because of this one Halloween outing she was locked in her room the rest of the year, only allowed out for school.

Hillary as a young girl was saddened and horrified by the ordeals that her mother would relate to her and it was these hard knock stories from her mother that instilled in her the need to champion the rights of and needs of children. As Hillary herself once stated, "Learning about my mother's childhood sparked my strong conviction that every child deserves a chance to live up to her God-given potential and that we should never quit on any child".

Clinton was encouraged by her mother's plight to make it part of her life's work to empower disadvantaged children, she sought out a way for the true best interest of a child, not just to put a roof over their head, would be paramount. The ill treatment of her mother, and the role the judicial system played in putting her in this precarious living situation with her ill-tempered Grandparents would be the template Hillary would use to construct a more just model of social services.

The courts of the 1930's although rightfully looking into the instances of domestic disturbance that Hillary's grandparents were having, did not have the wherewithal to find a suitable place for Dorothy to live after taking custody away from her mother. This was severe flaw in the justice system that the aspiring young attorney Hillary Clinton sought to fix. In her article for the Harvard Educational Review she wrote a piece entitled, "Children under the Law".

In this article she expounds upon the fact that in some instances children should have the right to decide custody themselves. The idea of holding a competency hearing, to determine if a minor is able to decide who gets custody of them was a rather novel idea at the time, but this is now common place. And despite the jokes about people divorcing their parents over doing the dishes and taking out the trash, the empowerment of minor's in tough situations, has become a cornerstone of modern social services. And enabling children in troubled living situations to have some say in where they wind up is common legal practice today.

Hillary was ahead of her time in championing this aspect of children's rights and the tough childhood of her mother was a major inspiration for her sagacity on this issue. If only her mother Dorothy could have been able to speak up and had a voice in the matter of her grandparents gaining custody of her, maybe things would have turned out different. These were the things that Hillary was fighting for as a fresh new attorney in the early 1970's.

Her crusade for children's rights would also come to define her tenure as the first lady of Arkansas. In 1983 Bill Clinton made Hillary Chairwoman of his "Educations Standards Committee". This was no minor task that her husband was having her take on, because when Bill handed the reigns over to Hillary Arkansas was at the absolute bottom of the educational barrel. She had her work cut out for her, and she immediately convened massive study panels to find the best way to turn Arkansas's faltering educational system around.

Upon taking office Hillary would attend over 75 meetings across the state and spend countless hours with her colleagues sorting through massive quantities of data about the state of educators and the educated in Arkansas. And in the process she made excellent strides in improving math and science curriculum and she had enough foresight and will to demand a mandatory kindergarten for the children of Arkansas.

She was known as a shrewd and determined operator and her ability to get things done led one legislator to remark, "It looks like we might have elected the wrong Clinton". But jabs at William Jefferson aside, she was a force to be reckoned with and a wise pick by Bill Clinton to head this committee. She introduced programs that were way ahead of their time such as the HIPPY program. And no, this program is not some throwback from Woodstock, HIPPY is an acronym which stands for "Home Instruction for Parents of Preschool Youth". HIPPY had it's origins in Israel but Hillary's inspiration for it came when she was visiting Miami, Florida.

Hillary was accompanying her husband the Governor on a "National Governors Association" meeting when the ever inquisitive Hillary came across a Miami Herald newspaper with the headline, "Mother's Get Lessons in Teaching". It turns out the headlining story was in regard to the work of a Hebrew University professor named Avima D. Lombard who was conducting research studies and programs that centered around directing parents to be their children's first instructor.

The program had originally been conceived by Israeli refugee advocates in 1969 who were trying to find new ways to help advance children with educationally and economically strained backgrounds. Well needless to say, when, Hillary Clinton, the former Yale Attorney that had spent years focusing on childhood education was intrigued, so she forked over the 25 cents, (or whatever a newspaper cost back then!) purchased the paper and the rest is history.

Hillary Clinton was a staunch advocate of this no holds bars approach to education, and the Clinton's poured much of their energy into that field during the entire tenure of Bill's Governorship. While many of Bill's advisor's cautioned him about rocking the education boat, and avoid upsetting teachers and the teaching establishment, Hillary encouraged her husband on, believing it to be a gamble that would pay dividends. Many in retrospect think that she was right in her all or nothing take on education, and point to the 1992 presidential election as Hillary's Jackpot.

Chapter 2
Two for the Price of One

The 1992 election year is one that I still vividly remember, in fact to just go ahead and throw a date on myself altogether here; it is the earliest election that I have any memory of. I was around 8 or 9 years old at the time. And thinking back to that time period, even from the perspective of an 8 year old, that election seemed like a big deal; and it was. Because it was a chance to put an end to three consecutive terms of Republican rule, a major changing of the guard in American politics.

Since the day I was born there had always been a Republican in power, two installments of Reagan and then the familiar monotony of the third Republican term of Bush senior. Been then 1992 happened, and suddenly there was a new contender and something about him seemed different. I was way too young to understand partisan politics and the supposed differences of party platforms such as Democrat and Republican, but I didn't have to.

Because even though it would be decades before I would earn my Political Science degree, even as a child I could perceive something about the man named Bill Clinton, with his flashy smile, and upbeat charisma that made him stand out. He stood in stark contrast with the much more reserved George H.W. Bush, who was famous for his bored yawns and glancing at his watch during heated political exchanges.

You didn't need to take a political theory course to see the charm of Bill Clinton, in him we had something different, and this Governor from Arkansas was ready to grab the whole world's attention. But Bill wasn't the only show stopper that election year, because it was Hillary Clinton who would capture the nation's attention more than any potential first lady in American history.

Bill Clinton often joked that the country was getting, "Two for the Price of One", but the jest was both true and prophetic in nature. The election and two terms of Bill Clinton was in many ways more akin to a co-presidency, an unofficial relationship similar in nature to the one said to have been shared between, John F. Kennedy and his Attorney General brother Robert Kennedy. It was "two for the price of one", but in yet another historic mirroring of the Kennedy partnership, the Clinton Co-Presidency would create a rivalry similar to the one that L.B.J. had of the Kennedy brothers. With Al Gore often dealt with as a third wheel in the administration, things could get a little bit tense.

Gore was often frustrated to find that any major suggestion he made to Bill Clinton ultimately had to be run by Hillary first before any true decision could be made. At first he just sloughed this off to a man consulting with his wife, but it soon became clear that it was much more than that, and Bill Clinton in reality was comparing notes and taking constant advice from his second in command, because for all intents and purposes Hillary took on the role of closest advisor, and just like it was with Bobby Kennedy and John. F. Kennedy, this close partnership often had the effect of shutting Gore out of major decision making.

But to Al Gore's credit, he took most of this in strike and tried to be understandable of the close political ties of Bill and Hillary and avoided most of the L.B.J. style bitterness; basically he just accepted it and tried to make the best of it. He even made it a habit to meet with the Clinton's once a week to have group discussions. The first true cracks in this triumvirate styled administration would begin towards the end of Bill Clinton's second term however when the Monica Lewinsky scandal broke.

It seems that Al Gore was sincerely offended by the President's behavior and began distancing himself as the time of his own bid for a 2000 Presidential campaign neared. This distancing then came to a head in an infamous interview with Diane Sawyer who when inquiring with Gore about the scandal, Gore commented on the President's behavior saying, "I thought it was awful. I thought it was inexcusable. But I made a commitment to serve this country as Vice President."

Then in typical "preachy" Gore fashion, the V.P. added, "It is our own lives we must master if we are to have the moral authority to guide our children." This public condemnation of the head of his former ticket came as a complete shock to Bill Clinton, when he heard the news he is reported to have exclaimed, "What the F*** is this about?!" A fairly inelegant knee jerk reaction, but Bill quickly recovered and actually phoned Gore later that same day to congratulate him on his announcement speech, telling him, "Good Job."

In the end just like the scandal itself, Gore's condemnation left the Clinton's un-phased and regardless of any critique of their marriage, their political partnership was stronger than ever and to gore's amazement the Clinton machine had its sights set for a new Goal, the newly vacant Senate seat of New York. Overshadowed by Gore's attempt at the general election, much of the world wasn't paying attention, but 2000 was also the year of Hillary's very first ever attempt at political office, she couldn't compete of course, with the all-out coverage of Gore's Presidential campaign, but Hillary's own rigorous campaigning would have an unseen impact on Al Gore, mainly in the form of contributions.

A lot of the money that Gore was counting on from big name donors was actually being siphoned off to finance the Clinton campaign. This created a rarely mentioned, but very real, financial split in the Democratic Party that election year that had Clinton loyalists fundraising like mad for Hillary taking a lot of valuable resources away from the Gore campaign. Gore had suspected that his benefactor's wallets were being poached for some time and he had this suspicion confirmed literally right under his nose when Hillary attended one of his fundraising events under the guise of campaigning for him, only to grab the mike and ask for donations for her own Senate race! Gore was absolutely shocked and dumbfounded by the audacity of this act.

Gore was also amazed at how quickly Hillary's husband had assumed his new role of "Campaigner in Chief". While Gore's campaign against George W. Bush lagged behind, awaiting its ultimate doom of miscounted "Chad's" and other obscure voting anomalies. Hillary's Senate race was zooming along at full speed, leading to her decisive victory against Rick Lazio winning her New York Senate seat with 55 percent of the vote. Not exactly a landslide, but a great finish for a first time run for office nonetheless.

Bill Clinton who had silently stood in the wings supporting her campaign was proud of her accomplishment and ecstatic to see that she finally had the chance to use her talent in political office. After decades of Hillary supporting his own political ambition he knew that it was now his wife's time to shine, she had wanted to run for office for as long as he had known her, in fact she almost gave it a try, about a decade previously. It was in 1990 when her husband briefly hesitated in his bid to run for his fifth term as Governor of Arkansas that Hillary first seriously considered running herself, and enthusiastically spoke with her colleagues about her political prospects.

But in the end she was ultimately persuaded that running so soon on the heels of her husband's administration would leave her with too much baggage. As excited as Hillary was about running for office, this idea of her husband's "baggage" would come to haunt her prospects of being a candidate herself for many years to come. This concept of having to wait out her husband's baggage could be what prevented an earlier Hillary Presidential bid in 2004, it seems that she would had to wait a few more years for Bill to pick up his junk from the baggage claims department.

Chapter 3
Decision 2008 and the Cracked Ceiling

Hillary Clinton had been predicted by many to be a solid front runner, a sure thing; so it came as quite a shock when she came into third place in Iowa. Hillary described the moment as excruciating and after her devastating defeat by the Iowan's she would not step foot in that state again for another six years. Iowa in the game of Presidential politics is a king maker and a king breaker, it is the first major battle ground for primary contenders. Now that Hillary is running again in 2016, Iowa will once again be the first state that she will stake her candidacy on.

But what exactly happened in 2008 to create such a historic upset? Almost everyone, even while Iowan's were busy casting votes; were sure that Hillary would come out on top. How did she trail so far behind so soon? Many say it was precisely due to the fact that everyone took Hillary's ascension for granted, that the Clinton team, and Hillary herself were lulled into a false sense of security. Since everyone was so sure of a positive result, she did not campaign as hard as she should of. If only Hillary had committed herself to in depth grassroots campaigning from the very beginning, much like Barak Obama had, she may have been more successful.

From the outset of the Iowa campaign Hillary had performed more like a celebrated guest speaker than a campaigner. While Obama and Edwards were out schmoozing with the locals, going to their hang outs, and personally talking to them about their needs, Hillary was stepping into auditoriums speaking for large crowds. It was good for sound bites, but she just wasn't connecting on the personal level yet like the other candidates were. She wasn't going to them, essentially they had to go to her, and that just doesn't work in the campaign world.

It was this lack of personal attention that made many in Iowa dislike Hillary. Roundly criticized for her absence from town hall meetings, one frustrated Iowan explained

Hillary's efforts like this, "It was a grass roots campaign. I waited a long time to make up my mind and when I decided to support Obama, I had not received a call from the Hillary group and I never attended any of Clinton's functions. That's important. We are used to getting invited to small groups."

Hillary did not utilize small in your face gatherings like Obama and Edwards, instead she toured the state like a professor on a lecture tour; this was not a good way to get votes. It is widely said that the main failure to take a more personalized approach was her campaign managers who ignored their local counsel in Iowa and instead followed their own agenda. This neglect of her own local management team in Iowa proved to be her undoing in 2008.

After the Clinton team realized how damaging their lackluster approach was they shifted gears and Hillary would be in full damage control the rest of the campaign. And then the town hall meetings began where Hillary fielded questions from the American public that ranged anywhere from healthcare, the economy and the battlefields of Iraq and Afghanistan. She answered these questions well and with a firm stoicism that was a trademark of the Clinton campaign.

But the most memorable question by far was not one that involved soldiers on a far flung battlefield. The question that would catch her off guard had nothing to do with politics, and international intrigue, the question that caught her off balance was a rather trite one from a local TV reporter who asked her, "What can you say to the voters of New Hampshire on this stage tonight who see a resume and like it, but are hesitating on the likeability issue, where they seem to like Barack Obama more?"

It was the "likeability" question that went right to Hillary Clinton's heart during the 2008 presidential election. It was a question that had plagued her incessantly almost like a schoolyard taunt. The common argument from constituents time and time again was that while they viewed her as qualified for the job, they didn't know if they "liked her enough". This rather childish kind of "Nah Nah na Boo Boo we don't Like you" sentiment could have been enough to get anyone down. But Hillary with her usually thick skin had previously taken such charges in stride.

It was not until this moment under the hot lights of the New Hampshire debate, when Hillary was made once again to contemplate just how much American's liked or didn't like her that her walls finally began to come tumbling down. And America began to see a more raw and vulnerable Hillary Clinton. Seemingly caught off guard, she immediately paused when she heard this question, and started to answer with a slow and measured statement, highlighting the difficulty of her campaign, and then more importantly the difficulty facing women today, she then empathetically intoned that elections were not, a "game" and then looking right into the camera, in front of millions of Americans, she began to cry.

Many were quick to jump on this moment for political purposes, claiming that this kind of "outburst" showed that Hillary was unstable, and political pundits began to write her off because of it, claiming that her voters would dismiss her because of this show of weakness. But no matter what the armchair and TV set politicians tried to say about it, the true verdict came out with the results of the New Hampshire primary. And in a state where she was initially failing to gain traction, suddenly the momentum was all hers, and it was this show of raw emotion that is credited as the moment that took Hillary over the top.

Because it seems that after years of picking away at her hard, iron surface they finally got a chance to see the real Hillary, and it turned out that, after some of the tough exterior was peeled away, this was a woman that they liked very much after all. Many remarked that it was when Hillary had let down her shields and had a bit of a breakdown, that they actually began to like her even more for it, and empathize with her. When that veneer of steel had been removed just for a bit, it turned out that she was someone they could admire, and yes, even like; after all.

And as Hillary's 2008 run came to a close, Obama made it clear that he liked her as well, and wanted her to have a place in his future administration. The Obama team had begun making overtures to her as soon as she made her concession speech, with many predicting that she would be made the vice presidential candidate on his ticket. Although, this kind of partnership did not end up materializing, Obama made his true plan for Hillary known immediately after his election. The post he had envisioned for her was not Vice President but Secretary of State.

This was a role for her that Obama was quite vocal about, repeatedly voicing his enthusiasm for it and telling her that she was simply, "the best one for the job". But even with all of this positive feedback, Hillary found herself hesitating to accept. While greatly flattered by the offer, and sincerely interested in taking up the post, she felt that she still had a lot of work to do as a senator in New York. So after a quick post-election meeting in Chicago to discuss the details, the ever pragmatic Hillary famously told Barack, "I'll think about it."

Chapter 4
When the Arab Spring was Sprung?

As much as President Bush had been roundly criticized for trying to create democracies in the middle east and for his constant calls of changing the "hearts and minds" of citizens of dictatorships all over the world, his administration was not the only one involved in the engineering societies. Hillary has revealed in her latest memoir "Hard Choices" that just after the overthrow of the long time Egyptian dictator, "Hosni Mubarak" her state department was busy trying to capitalize on the movement.

She recalls that just days after the event, a video was circulated in the region depicting footage of the then number two man of Al-Queada, "Ayman Al-Zawahiri". In the video Al Zawahiri is shown stating that, "Peaceful action will never bring about change in the Middle-East". Immediately after Al Zawahiri says these words the scene then fades to young Egyptians on the street in peaceful protest and then celebrating the fall of Mubarak, as if there riotous overthrow had contradicted the words of the terrorist.

At this point in time there was no way to know exactly what the outcome of Egypt's Arab spring would be, most observers filled to the brim with their idealism, had hailed the overthrow of Mubarak as a victory for democracy very early on. So to be fair to Hillary, there was no way she could have known the forces that would have been unleashed, but even so, in this situation, the normally pragmatic Clinton was unusually quick to put her seal of approval on the whole affair.

Videos like this coming straight out of the state department were early indications to the people on the streets of Tahir Square that they were being supported by the United States, and if any former dictator like Mubarak were to speak up and say, "Hey guys be careful! You don't know quite what you are dealing with!" Most of us would have tossed it up as the lies of a dictator. But today we know this story plays out much different, and is much more complicated.

Now we know that, even though dictators very well, do lie, they are also capable of telling the truth, and as ISIS is swarming over and threatening to engulf every single region that a dictator was removed from, the words of another former dictator come to mind, "its Al-Qaida! It's Al-Qaida! My people love me! They love me!" This is what Momar Kaddafi of Libya said shortly before he was liquefied by revolutionaries in the street. Until the very end he claimed that most of the agitators were being fueled by terrorist organizations.

And although we can with a good amount of certainty say that most of his citizens did not exactly "love" the cruel dictator, we can also see that Momar was at least halfway telling us the truth. His removal did in fact bring in Al-Qaida and other extremist elements, the latest of which is ISIS pushing in from Syria. With events in the Mid-East and North Africa getting worse and worse, with religious minorities (mainly Christians) being slaughtered in the thousands, the Arab Spring becomes something much harder to celebrate.

Hillary and the state department still stand by many of their decisions but many critics have raised a telling point. Many of us say we would like to see democracy in the Middle East, we say that we would like dictators thrown out with a leader selected by the people. But as the United States, the most powerful country in the world is championing this so-called democracy, it comes with an understated caveat; the democracy that we would most like to see, is one of our own design.

Above all else we would like to see a democracy that espouses ideals similar to our own. But we often forget that democracy in its raw form simply means, "Rule by the people". Sounds great but what if the majority of those people want to do bad things? What if there was a popular move to persecute religious minorities? What if 51% of this supposed democracy voted to remove all Christians from the land would that be a good thing? Of course not, but this is the strange truth of democracy and at its most base, uncontrolled level, it can in fact be dangerous.

Democracy needs to be nurtured and it needs a good constitution with civil protections and stewards that have been sworn to protect those rights. The Arab Spring of Egypt was not properly equipped with any of those safeguards and checks against mob rule that we take for granted in our own country, this is a concern that the Secretary of State would eventually give voice to.

Just a month before Mubarak's resignation she was at a speaking engagement with the state department in Munich, Germany where in reference to the ongoing events of Tehir Square, she issued out a stern warning against unchecked democracy, stating that while, "Free and fair elections would be necessary" but they would not be enough, and she then elaborated this point by saying, "Functioning democracies required the rule of law, an independent judiciary, a free press, and civil society, respect for human rights, minority rights, and accountable governance."

Hillary had the prescience to know that these fundamental building blocks of a fair and non-biased democracy would be needed to produce a place of peace and not just a conglomerate of mob and riot rule. These are the corner stones of a peaceful democratic state. If here in the United States we had to riot every time we wanted a piece of legislation or bill adopted, we would be in a lot of trouble. What the Egyptians needed more than anything was a solid foundation to build their democracy on.

But as Hillary toured the country in the days immediately after Mubarak's fall, this kind of foundation proved to be elusive. In fact when Hillary would inquire with Egyptian protesters or discuss with young college students at the University of Cairo, what their post-revolutionary plans were, and how they would rebuild Egypt, she just received dumbfounded stares, it was if the thought had never crossed their mind. So much energy had been expended in hurling themselves at a brutally authoritarian regime that no one had taken the time and consideration to think of what they would do next, once it had been removed.

While a frail military transitional government was in place Hillary toured the country trying to find answers, but was surprised to find mostly blame. It seems that once the original object of their rage, "Hosni Mubarak" had been taken out, many of the protesters began to refocus their discontent onto the United States, citing the U.S. as the primary cause of their suffering. And to Hillary's shock and amazement, she would become the most popular object of scorn from the U.S. administration.

I still remember seeing in the news, the picket signs and protest banners that sprouted up shortly after Mubarak's fall that screamed vitriol at Hillary Clinton. I was a bit dumbfounded myself about that one. I remember seeing signs that read things like, "Hillary must Go!" and the ever so popular slogan, "Down with U.S.! Down with Clinton!" I remember at the time that I saw all of these signs firmly denouncing Hillary, I thought to myself, "They know that she's not the President right?" It was strange that a Secretary of State was being so thoroughly blamed and solely held responsible for everything.

But even the picket signs that greeted her motorcade were nothing compared to her hasty exit when the cars in her convoy were hit with a nonstop mixture of tomatoes, shoes, water bottles and spit. And then to top it all off in her final send off the crowd got this ingenious idea to shout, "Monica! Monica!" a bizarre reference to the Monica Lewinsky scandal of 1998, and then as a final great flourish many of the people screaming on the side of the road pulled down their pants and shook their bare bottoms at the State Department's motorcade.

Is this democracy at work? I'm not sure how Hillary felt about it, but it must have been tragic to have a country she worked so hard to build up, collapse and then spew their rage and hatred on her. Even without the tomatoes and insults it must have been heartbreaking to see a movement that so many here in the United States beautified and idealized turn into something so ugly.

I remember when "Egypt's spring" began how inspired people were that young people turning to Facebook could start a revolution. And according to Hillary's book "Hard Choices" Obama's own aides were, "Swept up in the drama" and "Idealism of the Moment". But as these events can show us, even the loftiest of ideals, without a solid plan, can quickly turn into a rear end in your face.

Conclusion
2016 and Beyond

She has held many titles and been many places. And this well-traveled warrior cannot rest yet. Whether she likes it or not, the world expects her to run in 2016. When Hillary made her official announcement as a Presidential contender for the 2016 race it came as no surprise to anyone except perhaps herself. If you would have asked her two years ago if she was going to run for President, she would have told you "no".

But it seems that like many other times in her life, fate has a bigger power over Hillary Rodham Clinton than her own personal choice. Just like she was persuaded, convinced and cajoled onto that stage at Wellesley College all those years ago, she is equally being pressured by forces of persuasion beyond her control to mount the stage once again in 2016. It's a rendezvous with fate that goes beyond her own personal will, and Hillary Rodham Clinton is ready and willing to take up the call.

Review Link

If you enjoyed this book, we would really appreciate it if you could leave us a positive REVIEW?

P.S. **You can <u>CLICK HERE</u> to go directly to the book page** and leave your review and/or purchase our other books above. Alternatively, you can copy and paste this address into your browser --- http://amzn.to/1wCj3OE

CHAPTER 1
Are You Ready to Earn Big?

Being your own boss is a very rewarding career shift, taking control over your time, management preferences and finances. By being an online entrepreneur, you open more opportunities for you to achieve higher success and become someone bigger in the business world. The reality is, no one becomes a multi-millionaire just by staying an ordinary employee, solely relying on salaries and bonuses. There is no real financial independence to that.

The richest and most successful people in the world all have their businesses. Even Oprah Winfrey, the respected and richest celebrity in the world, did not reach Forbes 1000 list without her OWN Network, a media empire she built from scratch throughout the years of her hosting stint.

Just imagining the benefits of being your own boss already sets high expectations because the possible advantages are really endless, only bounded by how much time and effort you are prepared to allot on your venture, willingness to take risks and the ability to grow professionally, mentally and emotionally. All those benefits, however, are not without sacrifices - sacrifices that when done inappropriately can ruin you instead of giving you a better life.

Being your own boss means sacrificing the security that the corporate world has to offer. The steady paychecks become irregular, paid leaves and company-sponsored vacations become a personal expense, accountabilities become a sole burden and high-rise office building becomes a former storage room next to the kitchen and garage. All the perks of being a top employee will vanish all of a sudden as you step out of the corporate world, unless you can build your own corporation immediately. Of course, that does not happen right away, most likely, not even in the following months or years to come. Still, it is possible, and that is exactly your goal here - to start your own business empire - your own boss.

But how do you know if you are absolutely up for the challenge and cut to be your own boss?

First, you need to have a business concept in mind. Becoming an entrepreneur can be two things: a commercial business and a home business. A commercial business is something that you set-up the traditional way - store, location, customers, merchandise and perhaps, employees.

A home business can also have most of that, but you have the freedom not to. In fact, a home business can just be you and your customer. Either way, you need to have a solid business idea for your starting point. In the next chapter, the most in-demand, timely and successful start-up business and home business ideas will be presented to help you get your venture started the fastest way possible.

Second, you need to have savings or expected sources of business financing. Be prepared to shoulder everything. The capital is your startup cost that covers equipment, raw materials, utilities, taxes and everything that has something to do with your business operations, whether it is a piece of computer or delivery van. In the end, your ROI (Return on Investment) will depend on your capital, and that can take months or years to collect.

Third, you need to have security for yourself and your family. Investing in a business can bring instant financial success, but might also take months before you can see your first dollar. The mortgage will not wait. Loan amortization will not wait. Medicines and medical attention will certainly not wait. Unless you have enough savings to cover business and regular expenses for at least six months, then you can file your resignation letter and jump into the world of entrepreneurs.

Ensuring medical insurance beforehand and allotting a budget for emergency cases are important because risking your family's health, life and future should always be taken out of the equation. Even large corporations have buffer funds to access during financial crises.

If you think you do not have enough money to gamble on a business venture that may or may not work, the next best decision is to save your dream for another day, and hope that it will be better next time. Or better yet, start with a home business that needs nothing but your brain and guts to work.

Fourth, you need to have a plan, and that will mostly be covered in the chapters to come. There will be marketing, management and financing involved, and for someone who has not gained extensive experience in actual business operation, or has not been formally educated with the intricacies of running a business, all the tasks involved can be too overwhelming.

Lastly, you need to have the heart to start a new career. Like what has been said, starting a business is toiling through a new chapter of your life that includes so many sacrifices. Every second you spend on your new venture is a second taken away from yourself and your family. Hours of working on your newfound joy mean hours of missed opportunities to accompany your son to a baseball game, or watch your daughter dance on a musical. Or it can be hours of intimate conversations with your partner.

A balanced life is crucial because giving more weight to either your family or business can cause all your hard work to tip over.

If you like this preview, then *click here for the full story of this eBook!*

Or go to: *http://www.amazon.com/dp/B00XCBR6NS/*

Check Out My Other Books

Ultimate Guide to Financial Freedom
Achieve Wealth, Attain Success and Manage Your Debt like the Rich

Bodyweight Exercises
Training to Build Muscles and Lose Fat: Beginner to Advanced Routines to Strengthen Your Core

Wearable Technology
Discover 20 Trends and Interactive Mobile Sensor Devices to Include Children, Medical and Wearable

Productivity Power
Your Daily Guide to Habit Stacking, Preventing Procrastination and Forming Successful Skills

Books of author Ricky King
Gilgamesh: King in Quest of Immortality
An Extra-Biblical Proof for the Genesis Flood

Holy Land Collection
Israel vs. The World and Jesus, Jew & Jerusalem

10 Steps against Pornography
A Step Journey to Overcoming Internet Sexual Addiction through Jesus

Jesus, Jews & Jerusalem
Past, Present and Future of the City of God

The True Nature of Intelligence
Musings on the Ancient Sumerian Culture from a Christian Perspective

Israel vs. The World
The Apple of God's Eye in the End Times

Dedication

To our three blessings that have made RicTamily complete and continue to grow together in His loving embrace.

Disclaimer

The information in this book is in no way intended as medical advice. This book is not meant to be used, nor should it be used, to diagnose or treat any medical condition. The author disclaims responsibility for any adverse health effects that come in combination with the use of methods and suggestions presented in the book. The publisher and author are not responsible for any health or allergy needs that may require medical supervision and are not liable for any damages or negative consequences from any treatment, action, application or preparation, to any person reading or following the information in this book.

www.ingramcontent.com/pod-product-compliance
Lightning Source LLC
Chambersburg PA
CBHW050920290526

45792CB00002B/827